CONFIDENCE-BOOSTING STRATEGIES

for primary music teaching

SOUND BEGINNINGS

MUSIC TEACHING AT KEY STAGES 1 & 2

Richard Frostick

FABER *ff* MUSIC

Many thanks to Dr Dorothy Taylor
for her invaluable help and support
in the writing of this book.

Until I saw the sea is taken from *I feel the same way* by Lilian Moore.
Copyright © 1967, 1995 Lilian Moore.
Used by permission of Marian Reiner for the author.

© 2001 by Faber Music Ltd
First published in 2001 by Faber Music Ltd
3 Queen Square London WC1N 3AU
Illustrations by Harry Venning
Design by Nick Flower
Printed in England by Caligraving Ltd
All rights reserved

ISBN 0-571-51991-1

To buy Faber Music publications or to find out about
the full range of titles available please contact your
local music retailer or Faber Music sales enquiries:

Faber Music Limited, Burnt Mill,
Elizabeth Way, Harlow, CM20 2HX England
Tel: +44 (0)1279 82 89 82
Fax: +44 (0)1279 82 89 83
sales@fabermusic.com
www.fabermusic.com

CONTENTS

Foreword

As a primary teacher, you already possess many of the requisites for good classroom music practice. All the techniques described here can be acquired and developed by teachers who are not specialists in the field of music. It is hoped that this book will help primary classroom teachers to approach the latest National Curriculum guidance secure in the knowledge that they already possess a range of relevant skills—and confident in their ability to build on them.

In this book I suggest ways in which teachers can develop their practice from what they already know, understand and can do. It is intended for teachers who would like to increase the range of musical experiences available to their pupils but lack the necessary confidence, are unsure how to proceed, or who need reassurance that they are doing the right thing. (Trainee teachers, those at the beginning of their careers and parents may also find it of interest.) This slim volume is not a comprehensive manual of primary music practice, neither is it a complete set of lesson plans or a scheme of work! Rather, it is a reference book of teaching skills, and sets out some straightforward techniques for teaching the key elements of the curriculum.

Which Key Stage?

The prior experience of the pupils is of prime importance when considering what to teach. For this reason, age-ranges for the activities have not been specified, but a broad age-group will be suggested by the nature of the activity. The activity boxes, frameworks and games you will find in some chapters of this book are purely illustrative—the ideas within can (and are intended to) be adapted for use in a wide range of situations.

The National Curriculum

The terms and descriptions in the book are those used in the statutory programmes of study in the revised National Curriculum and in the non-statutory schemes of work. Although full compliance with the National Curriculum can of course only come after careful consideration of the statutory requirements, with the aid of this book, you will be well on the way to fulfilling the key elements of:

- **Performing** or controlling sounds through singing and playing
- **Composing** or creating and developing musical ideas
- **Appraising** or responding to and reviewing music

All three of these elements will encourage the children to **listen** and apply knowledge throughout their musical activities.

Pupils make progress by engaging with music in a number of ways. In the National Curriculum these are described as *Controlling sounds through singing and playing, Creating and developing musical ideas,* and *Responding and reviewing.* However, just as the elements of music present themselves to us simultaneously, so the ways of engaging with it are related and interact. For example, although in a classroom composing session creating and developing musical ideas may be at the centre of the activity, the pupils cannot but develop their performing and appraising skills as they work. At the same time they learn to listen and to apply their knowledge and understanding.

Focus your spotlight

In your music teaching be constantly aware that although a lesson might be focused on one particular musical element or feature, all the other qualities of the music will continue to present themselves and to interact with each other. For example, the exciting shark-attack music from the film *Jaws* creates tension through the combination of several different elements:

- The ominous depth of the first notes, i.e. **pitch**
- The unpredictability of its heavy accents and use of silence,
  i.e. **duration, dynamics**
- A crescendo, i.e. **dynamics**
- An increasingly busy
  orchestration,
  i.e. **texture** and **timbre**

The music from Jaws creates tension through the combination of several elements

Do not worry if you are not familiar with all these terms—a helpful glossary can be found at the back of the book. At this stage, the most important thing is to be aware that although we sometimes look at only one particular aspect of a piece, the music itself is expressive on many levels simultaneously. The integrated nature of the music curriculum is emphasized throughout this book. *The whole is so much greater than the sum of its parts.*

At every stage of your music teaching, ask yourself how the pupils' work could be better and how it could be developed. For example:

- When playing percussion and following your signals, are all the pupils watching?
- Does everyone slow down at the end, as required? Do they stop together?
- When singing, do they all sing the first word?
- Do they remember to sing the second line softly? Is it soft enough?
- Have they learnt the words of the second verse?

Don't let anything go if you think it could be better.

When improvements are achieved: praise, praise, praise! Because the skills required in music are not necessarily dependent on an ability to read and write, or even to speak, most classroom music activities are inclusive. They can offer opportunities for success—and therefore a chance to be praised—for pupils who may find it difficult to achieve or to be expressive in other media. The music teacher's task is to work out how best to use this natural advantage to the maximum benefit of all pupils, including those with marked aptitude. Where activities are less accessible to some children—the use of written symbols, perhaps, or certain movements—careful thought and consultation will be needed.

Remember that the best teachers constantly review and adjust their practice in the light of experience, just as we expect our best pupils to!

Don't worry if not everything goes exactly according to plan—it takes time to get things right. What is most important is that you develop an ability to look long and hard at your own work. If something goes wrong, consider some likely explanations and modify the activity accordingly. Ask some trusted colleagues for their views. Music teaching is a complex craft, but the rewards are huge! Read on …

Singing is at the core of musical experience and all musicians draw on their singing abilities to a greater or lesser extent. That is not to say that instrumentalists need to sing like Pavarotti or Ella Fitzgerald in order to make good music! However, an ability to perceive changes in pitch is essential.

Aside from pitch, so much else about music can be revealed through singing—harmony, rhythm, line and shape, variations in dynamics, sustaining tempo, the subtleties of timbre, to name but a few. Then there are songs: from the fourteenth century to the twenty-first; from all parts of the globe; in different styles, from blues to opera and from plainchant to rap, and the vast range of voices needed to sing in these styles. Then there is the physical activity of singing: learning how to breathe, to sing the words clearly, to 'place' the voice correctly, to blend with other singers and to be expressive. In short, singing encompasses virtually all elements of the music curriculum—not forgetting the sheer enjoyment factor.

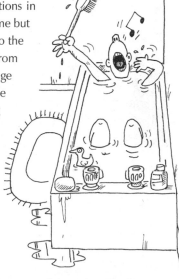

Making a start

Begin by getting acquainted with your own singing voice. If you are at all embarrassed, wait until you are on your own and experiment with your voice.

Remember that the aim is to teach the children to sing, not for you to give a concert.

If you are embarrassed, wait until you are on your own and experiment with your voice

Of course, the better you can sing the easier you will find it to teach a song, but the basic requirements are **an ability to sing in tune** and **a sense of rhythm**. Most people have these things—don't let them tell you otherwise! So …

Find a place where you are not overheard and sing anything. Find out the range of your voice: how high can you sing; how low? What kinds of sound can you make? Imagine you are teaching a nursery rhyme to the children: How uninhibited can you be? Could you mime some of the actions in the song? Experiment.

Encourage pupils to be inquisitive about their voices.

A C T I V I T Y

Singing can 'emerge' from other vocal activities, particularly in Key Stage 1. When telling stories about giants and elves, use giant and tiny voices. Ask the children about the giant's voice: is it low or high, loud or quiet? Who can do the best giant voice? What sound does the north wind make? Extend this approach to include songs. What do the monkeys playing in the trees sound like? What does the train sound like when it goes into a tunnel? What noise does the fire-engine make? Use movement whenever you can.

A C T I V I T Y

Play games with the class register: whisper the names and ask for the children's responses to be whispered. Enjoy the word 'whisper'. Then try opposites: if you read the names loudly the pupils must whisper in response, if you say them in a high voice, they must use low voices. Say two names loudly and one whispered all the way through; ask them what the pattern was. Sing their names to fragments of melody.

Some children may try to 'growl' the tune in your range

Choosing the right songs

One of the most challenging tasks for teachers is to find songs that inspire children and make them want to sing, but which are within their capabilities at the same time.

1. Choose songs that are within the children's vocal range
It is possible to sing songs in different keys:

Take a song you know and try starting from different notes.
Many of your starting notes will take you too high or too low,
straining your voice or even going out of your vocal range altogether,
but one or two will feel about right.
This means that you have found the right key for your own vocal range.

Finding a comfortable key for yourself, however, is only the beginning. What is comfortable for you may well not be right for your pupils, although most female teachers should be able to find some compatibility with the notes that their pupils can sing. Children's pitch-range is quite narrow and often lower then we think, so if they are having difficulty with a song, try it lower down. The golden rule is a simple one:
If there is undue strain for either you or the children, stop.

Most male teachers will naturally sing the tune in their deeper voices. In time, children get used to this and will automatically sing the song back in their own range. A few might find this difficult and may try to 'growl' the tune in your range. Adventurous male teachers could try teaching the song in a 'falsetto' voice, in exactly the same pitch as the children. Expect a certain amount of hilarity at first! This will settle quickly though, when the pupils realize that your efforts are helping them to sing the song more accurately. Once they know the notes you can revert to your natural voice.

2. Find songs that are appropriate to the ages and abilities of your pupils
Folk songs are ideal for children; their melodies lie comfortably in the voice and are a delight to sing. They also provide a musical social history of our own and others' cultures and are an excellent stimulus for project work. Tell the story of the song before you sing it, and make sure that the words are understood.

Many music publishers have collections of songs that have been selected by experienced musicians and teachers for specific age-ranges.

Some pop songs work well in the classroom, but you should handle their use with care. Children sometimes get very frustrated by their inability to match the sounds that they hear on their favourite recordings and will then mock any attempt to try. A little patient explaining about recording studios and techniques may help here.

Songs from the latest West End shows or Disney films often become very popular—there is usually a big ballad that becomes well-known.

For younger children there are numerous books of action songs. You can also make up your own actions or, better still, encourage the pupils to do so.

For very young children, take a nursery rhyme and make up your own words. You could turn *Three Blind Mice* into *Time for play*, or sing your own clearing-up song.

At all times, encourage the pupils to be expressive. For example:
- Is there enough variation in dynamics?
- Is the tone of the singing warm and round?
- Would any changes of tempo enhance the performance, for example, at the end of the last line?

Teaching a song

ACTIVITY

Sing the first phrase several times and ask the children to join in. When they are reasonably secure, sing the phrase once more with them and then continue with the second phrase on your own, without pausing. This can now be turned into a kind of 'call and response'. Ask the children to begin on their own and you answer with the second phrase. After a few repetitions, reverse roles, asking the children to sing the second line in response to your first.

With short songs you may not need to teach phrase by phrase. Sing a verse or chorus several times and invite the children join in.

By all means concentrate on one phrase if something needs correcting, but make sure that the overall flow of the song is not lost.

Take the most challenging rhythms from the chosen song and use them in some whole-class clapping and rhythm games (see *Performing Skills: Controlling Sounds through Playing*, page 14).

Chant the words with the rhythms, and then clap the rhythms alone. Use your hands to give indications of the shape of the melody: the higher your hand, the higher the note. You will find that infants and younger juniors will copy your hand signals; don't stop them—this will help them with the learning of the song. Once the chorus is learnt, sing the verse and ask the pupils to join in with the chorus at the right time.

Even at this early stage, strive to achieve as musical a performance as you can.

Explain that learning the pitch and rhythm is only the beginning. Experiment with variations in tempo, dynamics, timbre and numbers of singers. Encourage those who want to sing solo; once you have persuaded one child to be brave, they will all want to do it! Reward those who have the courage to do this.

Play games with the words: make up tongue-twisters, whisper lines, chant a verse in rhythm. The possibilities are endless!

Use an overhead projector for the words of the songs, or write them clearly on some sugar paper. It's better to avoid individual sheets—the children will tend to bury their heads in them.

Praise the children frequently.
Remember how vulnerable you
felt when you first started to
sing in front of them!

Praise the children frequently

Developing the singing

Encourage pupils to sit or stand so that their breathing can operate freely. This does not mean that they must be bolt upright with a tense, rod-like back—in fact this can be worse than slouching. Simply ask them to sit or stand so that they can breathe in and out comfortably. Explain that most people use only a fraction of their lung capacity in normal life, and that in singing they need more air than usual. Ask them to breathe in without raising their shoulders; this should immediately improve matters.

Avoid long breathing exercises—they are unnecessary at this stage and can
cause dizziness.

Sing quietly frequently: this will encourage the children to listen to their singing and will improve the quality of their tone. With young children the sound will often fall back into the throat and the pitch will flatten and tone harden. An expression of mild surprise—lifting the eyebrows—helps to bring the sound forward and brightens the tone. As singing becomes a part of your class routine, start each session with some gentle warm-up exercises. Play some vocal games or take fragments of the song's melody and do some preparatory 'call and response' work.

Insist on clear diction. Explain that mouths must be mobile and energetic—more so than in ordinary speech.

Mouth a line without voice and see who can tell you which line it is. Ask individual pupils to do this in front of the class. Tell them to imagine that they are on one side of a sound-proof glass sheet and that they have to communicate a vital message to the person on the other side by mouthing the words clearly: 'There's a lion behind you!', or 'You've won the lottery!'

Accompaniments

Don't let the lack of an accompanist deter you from singing with your pupils—some of the best choral singing takes place unaccompanied. If you want some support, guitars can be subtle accompanying instruments, or there are many songbooks that come complete with a backing CD. The piano is effective if played sensitively—played less well it can dominate singers and act as a barrier in communication between teacher and pupils. If you have been leading some percussion work with the class, see if the children can play some accompanying rhythms. Choose rhythms from the song itself. Similarly, take a few notes of the tune and transfer them to xylophones or glockenspiels. See if they work when played repeatedly while the children sing.

Trouble-shooting: What do I do if ... ?

... a number of children seem unable to pitch at all?

In the bad old days these children were called 'groaners'. There must be thousands of adults up and down the country who have been put off singing for life by being told to 'mouth the words', 'go to the back', or even to drop out altogether. Children understand these euphemisms and can be very hurt and discouraged by them. A moment's thought will reveal the unfairness of this approach. We would never (I hope) tell a child who was not yet a fluent reader that they mustn't read!

The best strategy is simply to proceed.

Over the weeks you will find that their pitch will improve. Remember that infants' sense of pitch will be at an early stage of development, so look for improvement over time.

... I really can't sing in tune?

Follow the above guidelines but use tapes or CDs for your examples (see *Listening to Recordings*, page 37). Many people who have difficulty with pitch in their own singing can hear very clearly when others stray from the note. If you can't tell if the pupils' singing is in tune or not, still encourage them to sing with the recording. Others on the staff will support you if you need help on some of the finer points. Those of you who have classroom assistants may discover that they can sing in tune. If you really want to sing in tune, how about a few singing lessons?

... a group of boys in my Year 6 class don't want to sing?

Handle with care! There will be a number of reasons why they think that singing is not for them, some of which will be due to social pressures that you will not be able to act on directly. First, make sure that the subject material of the song is appropriate (see *Choosing the right songs*, page 9)—*An English Country Garden* may not be a popular choice for reluctant eleven-year olds! Ask them how many male singers they can name—make it a game or competition to see who can think of the most. If you can find some recordings of football teams singing, play these—see if they can remember the reason for the recording. Talk about how exciting it can sound when a (predominantly male) football crowd breaks into song. Discuss the great male choral traditions in Wales and Russia, or barber-shop in the USA; find some recordings.
When one or two of them start to make an effort, leap in with massive praise immediately!

Ask if four or five of them would be interested in forming a band! Start a club for them. Remember that if the boys are 10 or 11 their voices may be starting to change and causing them embarrassment.

How shall I fit singing into a busy timetable?

Aim to have at least one substantial session a week, during which you could teach a new song or work in some detail on the songs that are already known. Supplement this with short bursts of singing—before or after breaks, before story-time, moving from one activity to another, at home time.

It is possible to find songs that are relevant to all areas of the curriculum; weave singing into the very fabric of your school day.

In music education the term 'performing' is applied to any activity that gives rise to musical sound. Children may learn to play simple song accompaniments or to perform pieces that they have created and developed themselves. However, even the most basic activity, such as learning to change from tapping to rubbing, requires a degree of performing skill.

Circle activities

Circles allow children to take part on an equal footing; the teacher has a clear view of the pupils and they in turn can see each other. Communication is direct and can therefore be more effective than in other seating arrangements. Most primary classrooms have some kind of comfortable sitting area, such as the book corner, so by moving the furniture a little, the children can usually be seated in this space.

Begin with activities that don't require musical instruments. Use the body as an instrument: once you have established some routines and made your expectations clear, the gradual introduction of instruments will seem part of a natural progression and not the trauma that many teachers fear it will be. Many of the activities that you will have led without instruments can be repeated with them, and pupils will learn from comparing the two experiences.

Teaching an activity without instruments leaves the teacher and pupil free to concentrate on the pattern.

This is not to say that the use of body-sounds is only a stage as you progress to 'proper' instruments: you and your pupils will be surprised at the musical potential in the simple hand-clap or click. There is an abundance of music that uses these simplest of resources to magical effect: play a recording of Steve Reich's *Clapping Music* and the point will be well made!

Using instruments

When you feel confident with circle techniques and your pupils have become familiar with the new routines, try introducing some percussion instruments. When introducing them for the first time your choice of instrument will depend on what you want to achieve. If you intend to try some of the rhythm activities outlined in *Games*, instruments such as drums, claves or woodblocks will give you the required clarity of sound. If your initial approach is based more on an exploration of the sounds produced by different instruments (timbre), then a range of pitched and unpitched instruments (see *Glossary*, page 44) might be more appropriate.

When you feel confident,
try introducing some percussion instruments

Games

Playing musical games is an effective way both to introduce new ideas and to support the learning of skills over time.

Try 'passing the parcel' (a small tambourine) to a steady beat. When the beat stops, the pupil holding the tambourine must play it. Younger pupils can tap, rub or shake (the listeners must identify which); older ones can play a short rhythm. Spend some time at the beginning of the game making sure that the tambourine is passed evenly. In the previous session you might have practised maintaining a steady pulse by sending a clap around the circle to a beat; once the first clap is half way round, start a second one.

Think of the games you play with your class already and see if you can adapt some of them for musical use. Enlist the children's help—when they've made up the rules themselves, they're usually better at keeping them!

The following activities can be used with or without instruments. To begin with, start and stop at what you consider to be the most appropriate points for your pupils. As you learn more about their musical abilities, adapt the activities accordingly.

Tap, Rub, Shake

Start tapping your shoes lightly and rhythmically with both hands and ask the children to copy you. Move up the body, tapping or rubbing. Stop whenever you want to point something out. When you change from tapping to rubbing, ask, 'What's different now?', or draw attention to the different sounds: 'Listen to the difference between tapping my hand and tapping my leg'. Shake your hands at the end, explaining that soon you will give them instruments to shake and that you want to prepare them for this.

Try the activity again in subsequent sessions but focus on a different musical element: for example, tapping very quickly or slowly (tempo), or starting quietly and increasing the volume (dynamics). Ask the children to describe what is happening. When you feel they are ready, introduce terms such as 'crescendo' ('gradually getting louder') and 'diminuendo' ('gradually getting softer'). Make up some words about tapping, rubbing and shaking, and put them to the tune of a well-known nursery rhyme or song (see *Choosing the right songs*, page 9).

Sing the following to the tune of *Frère Jaques*:
> I am tapping, I am tapping,
> Rubbing too, rubbing too,
> Shake a little, shake, shake,
> Shake a little, shake, shake,
> Tap your shoe, tap your shoe.

Later in the term, when you have introduced instruments to your class, repeat the activity. Build up a little band with drums, guiros and maracas. While six pupils play in the band, the rest of the class can sing the song, and all the children must tap their shoes at the end!

Development

On a glockenspiel, xylophone or metallophone, find the note C. Play it and count down four notes to the note G. Using one pupil, demonstrate to the class how to play C G C G C G all the way through the song as an ostinato (see *Glossary*). Then invite a small group to join in on their pitched instruments.

In subsequent lessons, develop your work on pitched instruments in the following way:

Clap 1 2 3 4 repeatedly and steadily, with a strong accent on the 1 and a slight accent on the 3. Then play C D E C, C D E C ('I am tapping'). Clapping again, ask them to copy you, but miss out the clap on the 4 and substitute a precise 'hands apart' gesture. You are now clapping 1 2 3 rest 1 2 3 rest. Next, practise playing E F G rest, E F G rest—'rubbing too'. Now repeat the C G C pattern, but with a rest—C G C rest C G C rest. This is 'tap your shoe'. (Don't try 'Shake a little, shake, shake' for the time-being—it's quite awkward to play.) Sing the song as a round, just as you would *Frère Jaques*. Ask the children to tap and rub with their singing, and discuss the result with them. You could even add pitched instruments to the round later.

Take a tambourine and stand where the lower half of your body can't be seen (behind a bookcase or low screen). Tap, rub or shake the instrument and see if the children can identify how you are playing it. Take two or three instruments and see if they can say which is which, or play two at once—the possibilities really are endless! Then ask a pupil or a small group to do what you are doing.

Give some advice on beater technique: keeping your wrists flexible, show how different sounds can be made by 'bouncing' the beater off a metallophone or leaving the beater on the note. Take a pitched instrument behind the bookcase and see if the children can tell which technique you are using.

Return to *Tap, Rub, Shake* when you have read *Composing: Creating and Developing Musical Ideas*, page 23, and set up a composing session using body sounds and instruments. Make up another tapping, rubbing and shaking song to the tune of *London Bridge is falling down*.

The Radio Game

Sit the pupils in a circle and place an unpitched percussion instrument in front of each child (try a mixture of tambourines, maracas, tambours, claves and guiros). Say that you are going to show them some signals: the first signal is a 'scooping up' movement with both arms, indicating that they must pick their instruments up as quickly and quietly as possible. The opposite signal is a downward movement with the flats of both hands, showing that the instruments must be placed quietly back on the floor. When the instruments are down the pupils must fold their arms.

Practise this several times, and praise those that pick up and put down with most control. You could prepare for this by asking them if they think you would be able to pick up a tambourine and put it down without making the slightest sound. Try it, and discuss the results. Then ask them to do it with their instruments.

For the next signal hold up the flat of one hand facing the pupils, like a traffic policeman indicating 'stop'. When they see this they must not play their instruments. When the hand turns round so that the back of it is facing them, they may make a continuous, gentle sound on their instruments. When the hand turns back, they must stop immediately. Tell them that the stop signal can come at any time so they must watch carefully! Show them how it works by doing the signals with one of your hands and playing a tambourine with the other. Vary the intervals between stops; have some very short bursts of sound—like a radio being turned on and off quickly. Now practise both pairs of signals with them—the pick up/put down and the start/stop.

Remind them that the sounds must be quiet and that they must watch your hands, not their own. This can be difficult for some children to begin with, but improves rapidly. When you see some particularly well-controlled responses from individuals, ask one or two to follow your signals, showing the rest of the class how important it is to watch your hands closely.

With the other arm, show the children another pair of signals. When it is by your side the sound must be as quiet as they can get it. As the arm rises up in a sideways arc away from you explain that they must gradually get louder, or quieter if it moves back towards your side.

Try these signals on their own, and then add your on/off (stop/start) signals with the other hand. Introduce the words 'crescendo' ('gradually getting louder') and 'diminuendo' ('gradually getting softer').

Development

See if the children can graduate the increases and decreases in volume so that they are spread evenly across the whole arc—if they get as loud as they can when your arm has only moved two centimetres from your side, they can't get any louder when your arm moves further. Talk about radios again; if the volume button makes the radio go very loud when it is only turned to '2', you need to fix the radio! Make sure that the correct descriptions are used—your arm is moving higher and lower, but the sound is getting louder and quieter (see *Glossary*).

Now catch them out: move the volume arm without turning the radio on with your other hand. Most of the class will play; some won't. Ask the ones that didn't to explain why. You can't turn the radio up if you haven't turned it on!

You can develop this further by asking a child to do the signals. Stick with the pick up/put down and on/off signals to begin with. When they are confident with these (maybe after several weeks), introduce the volume arm. Pair the children off around the circle: one does the signals and the other follows. Swap over. Some good pairs can perform for the class.

Be aware that both you and your children are developing conducting skills.

All Change

Clap a simple rhythm and ask the pupils to clap it back to you. Try to get your rhythm and the pupils' response to run continuously without missing a beat (see below). Without pausing, try a second rhythm, then a third: keep changing.

If you think that you don't know one end of a rhythm from the other, think again! Anyone who uses language uses rhythm, so go to language for the solution. Think of football teams or take some nursery rhymes and poems you know and choose some rhythmically distinctive lines such as *Tom, Tom the piper's son, One for my master* or *Polly put the kettle on*. Practise clapping four or five for use in the classroom. The three examples above fit neatly over groups of four beats:

Polly	put the	kettle	on
1	2	3	4

See if you can put an accent on the syllable that falls with the beat (Pol, put, ket, on). Hand the rhythm over to the children without pausing. Try the same with the other two examples above, then think of some others, varying the tempo and dynamics.

Development: don't clap!

Practise one rhythm with the pupils—this is the 'stop' rhythm. Repeat *All Change* with the pupils copying you as before, but when they hear the special 'stop' rhythm, they must not repeat it back (just like *Simon Says!*). Ask the pupils to play the game in pairs, taking turns to be the leader. Read *Composing: Creating and Developing Musical Ideas*, page 23, and return to the paired activity, asking the children to invent their own rhythms. Ask some pairs to perform to the whole class, and see if anyone can clap the 'stop' rhythm back. When you and the children are ready, try these activities using unpitched percussion.

Rhythm Sandwich

Begin by telling the pupils that you are about to teach them the most difficult rhythm in the world, then clap a single beat as steadily and evenly as you can for about twenty seconds. Ask them why this apparently simple activity is so difficult. If they don't understand, clap the beats again unevenly and see if they can spot the difference. Ask them to join in with you, clapping as evenly as possible. Say that you are going to make a 'rhythm sandwich'. Repeat the most difficult rhythm in the world, chanting 'bread, bread, bread, bread' with the beat. Ask one half of the group to clap and chant 'bread' slowly, and the other half 'butter' (two syllables to every 'bread'). Suggest some fillings—how about 'egg and bacon'?

Divide the class into three groups and build the sandwich like this, clapping and chanting at the same time:

1		2		3		4	
Egg	and	ba – con		Egg	and	ba – con	
But	–	ter _____		But	–	ter _____	
Bread _____				Bread _____			

Try 'cauliflower cheese' (they will love to invent disgusting fillings!).

1		2		3		4	
Cau – li	–	flower		cheese		[… wait …]	
But	–	ter _____		But	–	ter _____	
Bread _____				Bread _____			

Development

What variations can you think of? Using instruments, varying the dynamics, changing speeds? Divide the children into groups of three and ask them to invent their own sandwiches (composing). One can have the bread, a second the butter and the third can chant or play a filling of the group's choice. Read *Appraising: Responding and Reviewing*, page 32, and when they perform their pieces, ask questions such as:

- Who played the bread, the butter and the sandwich filling?
- Can anyone tap the rhythm of the filling?
- Did all the players begin together?
- How did the piece finish?

How about a melodic garnish to the sandwich? Can a recorder or keyboard player add a melody to the piece? Now that you have a plateful of sandwiches, how about trying to eat (hear) two or three at once? Is the class greedy enough to eat the whole plateful at once?

With all these ideas, try one five-minute session (or more if possible) during the day and combine these short activities with one or two longer sessions across the week.

You will be delighted at how the combination of 'little and often' and longer sessions supports the growth of your children's musical skills.

If something wonderful happens, show your excitement

Composing: Creating and Developing Musical Ideas 4

If you devise and lead activities in visual art, movement or drama, you are already experienced at encouraging children to create and develop ideas through the arts. In all cases an initial idea leads to the exploration of materials and their formation into an expressive whole. In music, children use instruments and their voices to create and develop ideas.

General tips for composing sessions

Use the circle–group–circle way of working whenever possible. The circle is ideal for initial explanations and demonstrations before moving into solo, paired or group work for experimenting and composing. Return to the circle for sharing work.

To begin with, try to stay in a circle, even when the pupils are working independently. Eventually, as you all gain confidence, you can ask them to move into other parts of the room. If the pupils become particularly absorbed in an activity, leave them to it. If they need more support, stop at intervals to give tips, share ideas or ask them to demonstrate a particularly effective piece of work to the whole class. Leave plenty of time to hear the pieces back. Encourage the pupils to comment on the music (see *Appraising: Responding and Reviewing*, page 32); maybe some of the individual pieces can be combined to form new pieces. Listen to the pupils' suggestions and try some of them out. If something wonderful happens (and it will!), show your excitement.

Record the children's pieces: you will then be able to keep track of their progress. Before each group plays, ask its members to announce their names, instruments and any title.

Notation

By using graphic notation you can show children clearly the link between sound and symbol. The principle behind it is very simple:

A piece for tambourine:

If you can play this you can read notation! See if the children can find ways of notating their own pieces (see *Responding through graphic symbols*, page 36).

23

The Lone Arranger

The Lone Arranger

Sometimes pupils learn fragments of songs and melodies on keyboards and other instruments at home and can be found in a corner practising these with great concentration and enjoyment. Often they will vary parts of the tune or rhythm, or add something of their own. By doing this they are following an age-old tradition in composition and improvisation! Ask them what they are trying to do—see if they can tell you what they are changing or adding. Find some recordings of themes and variations and jazz improvisations on well-known tunes. Tell them that they are in good company; the greatest composers would often take a well-known tune and write their own variations: Mozart, Beethoven, Liszt, Rachmaninov (there are numerous examples).

Devising composing projects

No book can ever hope to give a complete inventory of all the different possible approaches to classroom composing, and we should be grateful for that! The day that this happens will be the day that creativity is finally eliminated from the teaching process. Nevertheless, there are some strategies that are particularly fertile and can give rise to an exciting range of possibilities. Here are three Frameworks; each can be used repeatedly, using other musical elements as stimuli each time.

FRAMEWORK 1: The Island of Quiet

Project plan for investigating quiet and loud sounds

It would be fun to approach this through another subject, such as English, drama or movement. Ask the children to imagine an 'Island of Quiet'. Many years ago the citizens of this island got fed up with the loud noises that the giants made. They were nice giants, but so LOUD. The quiet citizens managed to trick the giants into having their own island, the 'Island of Loud', but every now and again a giant from Loud would come over to Quiet to see what was going on.

Seat the children in a circle and allocate instruments (see *Circle activities*, page 14). Using any instrument, demonstrate a range of techniques for playing quiet sounds. For example, on a tambourine you could tap quietly, change the sound by tapping with your fingernails, rub the surface gently, tap the metal cymbals, tap the wood, make a cymbal spin, shake the tambourine lightly— there are many possibilities.

Tell the children that you are a giant from Loud who has come to see what is going on. Before the children begin, remind them that they must 'freeze' whenever they hear your tambourine/drum/chime bar sounding loudly. Explain that it will be just like pressing the 'pause' button on a video. Demonstrate this by asking all the pupils to lift their instruments up and to make a continuous quiet sound. Say that you are going to try and catch them out. Play your instrument suddenly and loudly. Praise those that manage to stop immediately and are the best at 'freezing'.

Tell pupils that they have two minutes to find as many ways as they can of creating quiet sounds on their instruments. Say that you will be listening and looking for the pupils who can find particularly effective and unusual ways of making the sounds, and may ask them to play these to the rest of the class. They must remember that no one on this island is allowed to play loudly.

Ask the pupils to begin. Move around the circle supporting and advising. Give praise freely where it is deserved. Say that, as a giant from Loud, you are beginning to understand how pleasant some quiet sounds can be. If the noise-level begins to rise, stop the class and remind your pupils that they must play quietly.

At the end of the two minutes allow plenty of time to hear each pupil's sounds. Discuss the sounds with them: What does that sound like? Is she tapping, rubbing or shaking? Do you think you could play any quieter than that? Would that sound be good played with any others we've heard? What would happen if …?

Find some simple hand signals that you can use easily to indicate stopping and starting (see *The Radio Game*, page 18). Show these to the class and see if they are easy to follow, adapting them if necessary. Move around the circle bringing pupils in and out of the sound tapestry at will and discuss the result. Invite pupils to lead the piece with hand signals. Could the pupils be grouped according to instrument or type of sound? Get the children's views on this: ask them to suggest possible groupings.

The Loud giant is so impressed with the beautiful music from Quiet that he goes back to his island and tells all the giants how wonderful Quiet can be. The citizens of Quiet are sad to see him go because they are beginning to see how enjoyable Loud sounds can be. They start to visit each other's islands and soon they are all living together very happily.

Ask the children to imagine an 'Island of Quiet'

More ideas for lessons

Use other musical ideas or concepts as the focus for a lesson or project and then proceed in much the same way. For example, you could investigate:

- Gradually getting loud (crescendo) and gradually getting quiet (diminuendo), i.e. **dynamics**.
- Metal tuned percussion instruments (the 'Island of Metal'), such as glockenspiels and chime bars, inventing short, repeatable patterns, i.e. **pitch**, **duration**, **timbre**, **structure**.
- The sounds of wooden shakers, drums, bells, wood-blocks, i.e. **timbre**.
- Short and long sounds, i.e. **duration**.
- How the instruments sound in different numbers and combinations, i.e. **texture**.

FRAMEWORK 2: Until I saw the sea

In this, and in all projects that use poetry as a stimulus, encourage your pupils to perceive music as more than just a collection of sound effects. Initially, some of their pieces may sound like attempts to give the most accurate imitations of sounds. For example, in a project on 'A Haunted House', simple tapping on wood might represent the sound of mysterious footsteps on wooden stairs. Point out that a sense of mystery can be created in less direct ways; by a less literal translation of the story, or through the addition of other instruments to help create a feeling of tension. Illustrate this by contrasting recordings of actual sounds and musical evocations of them. Play a video or audio recording of fireworks and then play a recording of Claude Debussy's piano prelude *Feu d'artifice*. Discuss what you have seen and heard.

For 'A Haunted House', simple tapping on wood
might represent the sound of mysterious footsteps

Take a poem, or part of one, and discuss it with your pupils. Draw their attention to key words and phrases and ask for their views and impressions. Let's take an example:

Until I saw the sea
I did not know
That wind
Could wrinkle water so.
I never knew
That sun
Could splinter a whole sea of blue.
Nor did I know before,
A sea breathes in and out
Upon a shore.

LILIAN MOORE

- Take one phrase, such as 'wind could wrinkle water so'. Discuss what wrinkled water might look or sound like. Which instruments can evoke the 'wrinkling' of water most effectively? Which sounds and techniques work best? Try some alternatives.
- How could the sun 'splinter a whole sea of blue'? Experiment with instruments and techniques that might capture this effect.
- Repeat the experiment with 'a sea breathes in and out upon a shore'. Could the music of the wrinkling water, splintering seas and breathing waves be combined in some way?
- What if someone were to speak the poem with the music? What would the voice sound like in combination with the other instruments?

When the children's pieces have been performed, play recordings of music inspired by water (see *Before or after?*, page 37), such as Bedřich Smetana's *Vltava*, Fleetwood Mac's *Albatross*, Benjamin Britten's *Sea Interludes* or Franz Liszt's *Les jeux d'eau à la Villa d'Este*.

Work in a similar way with other starting points:

- Use a published story or one that a pupil has written. Alternatively, look at a painting or other work of art; again, these could be the children's own.
- Scenes from films or TV programmes often make deep impressions and can stimulate vivid pieces of music. Next time you hear a child giving a lively verbal description of something they have seen, ask how the excitement could be captured in music. Which instruments? How would they be played? When your pupils make up plays or are involved in drama, encourage them to invent music to complement and enhance their work.
- Take a cue from seasons, annual celebrations and festivals; Christmas, Halloween, Eid, May Day, Guy Fawkes, Diwali, Chanukkah, for example. Choose a poem or story about an aspect of the celebration or give the children free reign to make their own connections.
- Use the subject of a song they've sung. Perform the song alongside the children's pieces.

FRAMEWORK 3: The Planets

The Planets is a set of orchestral pieces by Gustav Holst. Holst portrays the planets using their individual astrological characteristics: Mars as the 'bringer of war', Jupiter as the 'bringer of jollity', etc. Without mentioning Holst's music, discuss with your pupils whether or not they think it would be possible to 'paint' a picture in sound.

- In a circle, introduce the names and descriptions of Holst's planets, still without revealing your source. Write them on the board or display them in some way.
- Experiment with different instruments and playing techniques and decide which sounds give the most effective impressions of individual planets.
- Choosing one planet, lead a piece with hand signals, using various combinations of sounds to create the desired effect. Discuss the result.
- Divide the class into groups of four or five and give each group a planet to portray. Have one or two of the planets worked on by more than one group; it is always interesting to contrast two treatments of the same idea.
- At this stage, see *General tips for composing sessions*, page 23, and proceed accordingly. After the pupils' pieces have been performed and discussed, introduce *The Planets* for the first time (see *Before or after?*, page 37). Draw comparisons between the pupils' work and Holst's music.
- Listen to recorded music that has similar associations, such as *Also sprach Zarathustra* by Richard Strauss (used in the film *2001: A Space Odyssey*) or David Bowie's *Space Oddity*.
- Work in a similar way using other pieces of music. Examples include: *The Four Seasons* by Antonio Vivaldi, *The War of the Worlds* by Jeff Wayne (based on H G Wells's novel), *Cats* by Andrew Lloyd Webber (try reading the children some of T S Eliot's poems from *Old Possum's Book of Practical Cats* first), *Pictures at an Exhibition* by Modest Musorgsky (compare recordings of the original piano pieces, the orchestral version, the synthesized version by Tomita and the rock version by Emerson, Lake and Palmer), *Carnival of the Animals* by Camille Saint-Saëns, and Claude Debussy's *Préludes* for piano.

Getting it right

In this kind of creative work it is generally better to challenge the pupils' perceptions over time rather than to suggest immediate solutions. *Aim to encourage and stimulate debate rather than to provide definitive answers.*

Art will always be controversial: if you can encourage your pupils to discover the world of musical invention and to discuss their work in an informed and thoughtful way, you will educate them well.

5 Appraising: Responding and Reviewing

Children respond to music in a variety of ways. When performing or improvising, a pupil will be creative in response to other musical stimuli; a solo improvisation will evolve and change in response to other players, or children will sing more loudly to compensate for an over-enthusiastic accompanist! These 'split-second' musical responses are skills of performing and composing, and are discussed in their relevant chapters. Other ways of responding to music, such as through speech, drawing, movement or by creating and performing other music, are considered below.

Encouraging verbal responses

ACTIVITY

Be aware of the skills that you use all the time in other subject areas. Think of some of the poems and stories that you have discussed with your class, and see how many of your questions could be transferred to a discussion about a piece of music.

Sometimes discussions can develop into basic exchanges of opinion that have little to do with the music! When you ask the vociferous pupil why they hate song x, they will either give non-musical reasons (the pupils playing it are not their friends, or the pop group wear silly clothes) or they will not be able to explain their views. If this happens, next time try the following approach:

Begin with just one golden rule—no sweeping judgements!

Tell the children that at the moment what they like and dislike is not your main interest. Rather, you want them to concentrate on what is actually happening in the music. Once your pupils have developed their listening skills and have acquired the use of some appropriate terms, they will then be able to support their preferences with informed observations. Make it a rule that no one is allowed to voice an opinion without a musical justification.

Not allowed:
'I don't like it—it's stupid'

Allowed:
'The chorus is repeated too many times—I got bored with it'

Children respond to music in a variety of ways

Prepare some straightforward questions for your pupils to answer: don't start by saying what the music is or who is performing it; just ask that the pupils listen attentively and answer the questions. Over the weeks they will come to expect surprises; you will be able to play them anything and they will be responsive. The questions can be changed to suit the age-group you are teaching and the language can be adapted—it could even take the form of a quiz:

- Does the music begin with one instrument, several or many?
- How many times is the first tune played?
- Which instrument plays the short rhythm that repeats over and over again?
- Does the singer start at the very beginning of the song or is there an instrumental introduction?
- Which instrument is playing when the singer sings the words …?
- Are there any stringed instruments playing?
- Is the singer unaccompanied at any time?
- Which instrument is featured more than any other?
- At the end is the music quiet, moderately loud or very loud?

If the music has been composed by pupils, the same kinds of questions can apply:

- Which two instruments played this rhythm (tap it) all the way through?
- Who can tap this ostinato rhythm?
- Did the piece begin very loudly or very quietly?

Pupils may wish to respond to the way in which the piece is performed. Encourage them to notice each other's skills as well as those of famous recording artists. Once your pupils are focused and attentive to the music, ask some questions about its expressive aspects:

- How does it give you the feeling that you are on a train?
- Why do you think this piece is called 'Snowflakes are dancing'?
- Why is everyone tapping their feet to this song?
- How does the composer make the piece war-like?
- Would it be war-like if it was quiet all the way through?
- How does the choice of instruments make a difference?

Hearing the pupils' impressions

It is very important to give pupils the opportunity to discuss how music affects them. Take your lead from the visible reactions of the children—if there are signs of excitement, ask some individuals to tell you about their feelings of fear or amusement. This will very often encourage others to talk.

Many children will want to tell you their imaginings in detail. You will hear of the empty cottage in the wood, the howling wind and of all kinds of situations and events. Although we might be able to say with some authority that the composer had not intended to portray this story (don't say that to the child!), the effect of the music may well have stimulated the child's imagination in this way. Let them talk. See if you can encourage them to make links between events in the music and their stories.

Children may want to talk about their personal emotional reactions to the music. Be calm and unfazed; tell them about a piece of music that makes you laugh or feel sad. Through your behaviour they will learn that it is normal to experience emotions in response to music.

Other vocal responses

Infants will often give non-verbal vocal responses to music. Music about animals will make them want to make animal sounds; similarly, music about transport will induce the sounds of trains and car horns. Take your cue from them and hear some of their sounds. Talk about them. Move into a song about animals, or a composing activity.

Responding through movement

Again, begin by thinking of all the ways that you already use movement in your teaching. Teachers of infants are particularly skilled at encouraging children to respond through movement and use it routinely as an integral part of their technique. Action songs help children to acquire a range of performing skills and the combination of singing and movement helps to deepen their knowledge and understanding of musical elements.

Infants will often give non-verbal vocal responses to music

Use gesture in all aspects of your teaching (see *The Radio Game*, page 18) and encourage it from the children.

(see *The Radio Game*, page 18)

ACTIVITY

If you are introducing them to a series of notes that rise steadily in pitch, step by step, show them the steps with gestures. If you want them to sing a line more smoothly, draw a smooth curve in the air as you sing. Crescendo and diminuendo can be indicated by your hands moving further apart and closer together. Younger children will copy you quite spontaneously; praise those who produce the best gestures.

Look at the songs that your children already sing and see if you have explored all their potential for movement. As well as the more obvious actions, like marching to *The Grand Old Duke of York*, look at songs that tell stories and introduce elements of movement, dance and drama. When listening to recordings look for similar opportunities.

Younger children will quite unselfconsciously make abstract movements in reaction to music. During crescendos they will make gestures indicating growth and they will make short, spiky movements to match a similar passage of music. Build activities from these impulses, like 'John spread his arms wider and wider when the music got louder. Let's stand up and see if we can make ourselves bigger when the music gets bigger/louder and smaller when it gets smaller/quieter'.

All children will move naturally to music with a strong, steady beat. If they start to move to a pop song, challenge a group to come back at break or after school to work out a more formal dance routine. Other kinds of music will inspire other kinds of dance. When listening to a piece of music, ask for signals to mark certain musical events, such as 'Raise both hands every time the trumpet plays' or 'Nod your head twice when the sitar comes in'.

Responding through graphic symbols

As a technique, this can be adapted for use in a variety of situations (see *Notation*, page 23).

A C T I V I T Y

Take a tambourine and play a range of different sounds,
asking your pupils to draw the shapes and symbols
that best represent the sounds.
The result is called a graphic score.

Compare and discuss the results. Move into a practical composing session and develop the idea.

Reviewing

The process of reviewing is one that any teacher will be familiar with and is referred to throughout this book in one form or another.

Any engagement with music brings with it an opportunity for review ...

... and in turn the possibility of progress. Central to this process is the ability to respond; as these skills are refined and developed, so reviewing can become increasingly astute and supportive to learning. If pupils hear a recording of themselves singing and feel that the tempo is too slow, they can record it again, singing at a faster speed. In a composing session where a group of pupils are working on a piece about a robot and decide that their instruments are not sufficiently metallic, they can try new ones until they get the desired effect. When a class hears a piece of music again, a number of pupils will begin to notice more detail. Keep recordings of your pupils' composing and performing and ask them to listen to their pieces some weeks later. They may decide to change nothing, or they may make improvements. What they will certainly do is develop their ability to listen, respond and review.

Listening to Recordings

As far as resources will allow, try to make sure that your audio equipment is of good quality. In order for your pupils to perceive detail in their listening, a clear, balanced sound should be audible from all parts of the teaching room.

Before or after?

If you intend to listen to recordings in connection with your composing project, consider carefully whether to play the extracts before or after the children have created and developed their own ideas. There are good cases for both strategies. By playing the piece at the beginning of the project you are setting the scene and stimulating the imagination, but it is sometimes difficult for pupils to be inspired by classroom instruments when they have just heard a full symphony orchestra! It is also sometimes interesting to begin composing projects without having heard other composers' ideas. Try both ways and compare the children's reactions.

Avoid talking over the top of the music. 'The elephant's tune will be coming in any second—get ready—there it is!' will obliterate the important ten seconds of music leading up to the tune. Instead, try 'When I raise my hand like this the elephant's tune will be starting' before you play the extract. Next time you play the piece ask the pupils to raise their hands when the tune comes in. If you are using questions to help focus your pupils (see *Encouraging verbal responses*, page 32), read them through before you start the music.

What to play

Begin with music that you know. Not only will you be able to teach with authority, your enthusiasm for the music that you like will be obvious and will catch the pupils' interest. Because your favourite music is alive for you, you will be able to bring it alive convincingly for the class.

Nothing aids communication more than enthusiasm.

Whether your interest is dance bands of the 1940s, fourteenth-century plainsong, Bob Dylan, *bel canto* opera, West African drumming or ABBA, don't ever think that any music is too dated, too esoteric or too eccentric to be interesting and educational.

Children enjoy surprises; be as wacky as you like—they'll love it!

You may also teach them the valuable lesson that it is OK to be unfashionable or unusual and to stand up for what you like. Be brisk and positive. If you begin apologetically—'I know this is a bit old, but The Clash were very big in my day and I think you'll really enjoy this'—all will be lost. Encourage your pupils to listen to all music with an equal respect and attention to detail.

Background information

Once the music has been heard and there has been some discussion, you can then give out information about its style and context. Be anecdotal—tell your pupils about the rock concert, party or Prom concert where you first heard it.

Give the children information about the performers; how they lived, musical influences, dress fashions, historical or social context, etc. Own up to the five-inch platform boots you wore to their concert, or the green streak that was influenced by the lead singer's hairstyle.

Let the children see that music is part of social and cultural phenomena.

Be anecdotal!

Pass the CD/record/tape cover round so that they can see a picture of the performers and read a bit about them. Find other materials—contemporary magazines, newspaper articles, photographs or even videos—and share them with the class. Bring in any souvenirs that you may have—a concert ticket, programme or photographs. Talk about other pieces of music of the same genre and play some of them. If you can, trace some of its influences through to the present day.

Developing the listening sessions

Once you have established a pattern, ask your pupils to bring in recorded examples of their own favourites and to present them to the class as you did; information about the pieces and performers, social and historical context, opinions and impressions.

- Group your sessions around common themes. You could choose a particular genre, such as film music, or an individual artist, a composer, an historical era—there are numerous possibilities. See if you can get your pupils to become aware of some of the characteristics that distinguish the chosen theme: 'We've listened to film music for five weeks and heard soundtracks from eight different films. Is there anything we can say overall about music for film?'
- Choose from the many excellent multi-purpose CDs that are now available. On the same disc you can now get audio recordings for whole-class listening combined with interactive CD-ROM software for information and extension work.
- Start to be more adventurous in your own choice of listening. After all, we are expecting the children to be!

There may be times when you feel it appropriate to listen to a piece of music with your pupils without any preparation or comment and without any expectation of a response. Let the children relax and put their heads down if they want to, and enjoy favourite pieces of music again and again.

7 Complementary Strategies and Activities

Setting up a music area

Good visual displays will show that you mean business.

- Visit local music shops, including record stores, and ask for any posters that they might not need.
- Establish working relationships with publishers; look at their websites or send for catalogues, stating what your particular interest is. Use the pupils' own work in your display wherever possible—this may be art, or written work with a musical theme, such as a poem or a piece of imaginative writing.
- At both Key Stages let your display reflect a broad interest in sound. Encourage pupils to see musical potential in everyday objects—sticks, shingle, shells, rubber bands, kitchen utensils etc., and include some of these in the music area. Make visual links between these objects and their 'proper' musical counterparts, e.g. sticks/claves, shingle/maracas, etc.
- Making musical instruments is an excellent way to interest children in the principles of sound, and the resulting maracas, drums, musical mobiles, and the like, make exciting displays as well as being of practical use.
- If you have classroom percussion instruments stored centrally ask if you can borrow some to put on display. Borrow a violin or trumpet from the school band and have an 'Instrument of the Week'. Show photographs of pupils performing in school concerts, musicals or shows.
- Have a close look at your school's book stock and arrange a small display of books about music. Show texts that have examples of notated music; pupils may not yet understand the notation but you will stimulate curiosity.
- Show cross-curricular links in your display, for example a project on India, a focus on Tudor history, or a study of the science of sound: refer to their musical aspects in the music area. Display a selection of CDs and tapes, and encourage pupils to bring in examples of recorded music that they listen to at home.
- Involve parents and families wherever possible (grandparents can be a wonderful source of material). A concert programme from the '80s, a photo taken at a rock festival, an autograph of a famous musician: all can excite interest and stimulate learning.

Carrying out research

Organize pupils into pairs or groups and ask them to research specific topics using books and the full range of media available to them. You will need access to a computer with either speakers or headphones in order to get the most out of software and the internet. CD-ROMs can be a particularly rich source of information and websites can offer pictures, text, audio recordings and video footage. With all ICT, allow time initially for free exploration and listening: this will give pupils a chance to become familiar with the programs.

Here are some ideas:

- As well as collecting and classifying information from CD-ROMs and the internet, pupils could wordprocess a poster or flier, make a recording, formulate some questions about a topic and create an interactive display.
- Give groups selections of percussion instruments and ask pupils to classify them according to type—material of construction or playing technique, for example. Allow them to handle the instruments.
- Ask them to devise a way of presenting their findings clearly, using either a written tabular form or a database. Invite the rest of the class to ask questions that the group must then answer using their chosen method of recording: How many instruments are made of wood? Which instruments could you play a tune on? There are simple databases available intended specifically for this kind of educational use. Use the same research method for other surveys.
- The same kind of database could be used to classify and store information that the pupils find on CD-ROMs. Commission surveys from the pupils. Ask them to find out the class's 'top five' popular songs, or to investigate the general listening habits and preferences of other pupils and their families. Collect the results on a database and display them in the music area.

Involving professional musicians

Most British orchestras run education projects and would be pleased to talk to you about ways that your pupils could become involved. The professional animateurs leading these programmes are usually very experienced and of high quality; your children will have a wonderful time and you will pick up all sorts of tips. Make sure that you are on the mailing lists of local concert halls and theatres; information about educational projects is often contained in their fliers, or you could try their websites. Your local authority may well support projects involving professional musicians.

If you are sent details of groups that you have not heard of, speak to teachers from other schools who have used them. If the group can't give you references, don't get involved.

Human resources

See yourself as a resource! Most of us have some kind of interest in music and have experience of it in one way or another. Tell your pupils about concerts you've attended or new CDs that you've bought, sharing musical experiences with them as a matter of course. The children will already have a range of listening experience drawn from a number of different sources—television, radio, film, their own tapes and CDs, and those of other members of their household. They are usually very willing to talk about their likes and dislikes, and will often have extensive knowledge of their favourites.

See the pupils' families as a resource. Find out which parents play musical instruments and invite them to give demonstrations to the children. If your class

Involve families—grandparents can be a wonderful source of material

contains representatives of a range of cultural heritages, your parent group could be a particularly rich source of information and ideas.

Don't forget your colleagues! Ask around the staff room; you'll be surprised at how many teachers have musical skills and sing or play in ensembles. See if you can persuade them to perform for the children or to give a short talk about their musical instruments.

In most classes there are pupils who learn musical instruments, either in school or out. If you have, for example, several recorder players, invite them to play to the class individually or as an ensemble.

Developing your work

Contact your local authority; where there is no music adviser and no training scheme, ask for details of recommended in-service training providers. Many university departments of education and teacher training establishments run courses for serving teachers. There are a number of excellent independent organizations that run courses of good quality. Ask your Headteacher if he or she knows which schools in the area have classroom music that is considered to be particularly strong. Get to know good practitioners; most will be only too pleased to recommend courses and to share ideas with you. Looking at good practice is a wonderful way to learn—see if you can find a way of observing experienced music teachers in other schools or at workshops and conferences.

Glossary

Accent a sudden increase in volume on one particular note, indicating a stress.

Beat see 'duration'.

Crescendo/diminuendo gradually getting louder/gradually getting quieter.

Claves two chunky wooden sticks, tapped or rubbed together.

Composition the process of creating a piece of music.

Duration longer/shorter—including pulse, beat and rhythm. The terms 'pulse' and 'beat' can both be used to describe the recurring 'foot-tapping' emphasis that runs through rhythms, but 'beat' is now used more to describe the balance of strong and weak beats that form the 'pulse'.

Dynamics louder or quieter sounds. When working on 'louder' and 'quieter', watch out for the inevitable increases in speed when you get louder, and vice versa. Again, this takes time to get right. Correct the error by showing the children that you can get quieter without getting slower (make the sound of a ticking clock and ask them to imagine what would happen to the sound if they moved further and further away from it) and look for a steady improvement over time.

Guiro a hollow wooden instrument, shaped like a torpedo! Sound is created by rubbing its serrated surface with a stick.

Harmony the combination of several notes sounded simultaneously to produce a chord.

Improvisation the creation of a musical work as it is being performed, or 'making it up as you go along!'

Orchestration the combination of instruments or sounds. The word 'instrumentation' can also be used, literally meaning the different instruments for which a piece is written.

Ostinato a rhythmic or melodic pattern that is repeated throughout a piece or section. The rhythm games described in Chapter 3 are based on patterns or ostinati created by clapping.

Pitch higher/lower. Children often mix up 'high' and 'low' with 'loud' and 'quiet'. The numbers on volume controls—a higher number representing a louder sound—add to the confusion! Other difficulties sometimes arise from moving to the right to go higher on a keyboard, and vice versa. When you think about it, these confusions are perfectly understandable and even rational: to a young child, 'high' and 'low' are vertical measurements. The best way forward is to gently correct them when they get it wrong; just point out the pair of opposites (link this with a session in literacy?) and persevere. Over time, and through musical experience, the concepts will settle in. It is generally not a good idea to attempt lengthy verbal explanations of these distinctions with very young children.

Pitched and unpitched percussion percussion instruments are usually labelled either 'pitched' or 'unpitched'. 'Pitched' percussion instruments are those which are tuned to different pitches, to the extent that you can play a tune on them; examples include xylophones, glockenspiels, metallophones and chime bars. 'Unpitched' percussion instruments are generally not tuned to a specific pitch; examples are some drums, tambourines, castanets and maracas. Be warned, though, that classification of this kind is not a precise science! Most instruments, even unpitched, will give out some kind of pitch when struck and others such as kettle-drums (timpani) are tuned according to the requirements of the piece of music they are needed for. Nevertheless, these descriptions can still be helpful.

Pulse see 'duration'.

Rest the absence of a sounding note, i.e. silence.

Rhythm the grouping of musical sounds by duration and stress. The description of rhythm as 'a pattern in sound' can be helpful. Show the children anything with a pattern (wallpaper, T-shirt or picture) and discuss what the pattern is and how it is repeated: illustrate this musically by clapping a short rhythm.

Structure different ways in which sounds are organized. Structure refers to the way that a piece of music is put together. A 'round' is a structure—sing one with your Year 4 pupils and discuss what is happening. If a melody is repeated in a song or instrumental piece, this is how the composer has 'structured' the music. Once you start listening to the way that music is put together, patterns of structure will emerge.

Tempo faster/slower. Use the word 'speed' as well as 'tempo' (plural 'tempi'). Watch for confusion when investigating dynamics (see above).

Texture different ways of combining sounds. Texture is generally described in terms such as 'thick', 'thin' and 'dense', and refers to varying quantities and combinations of sounds. A solo violin melody moving into a passage for full orchestra is an example of a thin texture changing to thick.

Timbre different types of sound. Play a note on a keyboard and then sing the same note. The listener knows which is the voice and which the keyboard by the quality, or 'timbre', of the sound. One voice can make sounds in a wide variety of timbres, as can individual instruments.

Tone sometimes used instead of 'timbre', this can also describe more subtle variations in vocal and instrumental sound.

Recommended Reading

A Scheme of Work for Key Stages 1 and 2. Music (QCA, 2000)

Adams, Pauline. *Sounds Musical*. Key Stage 2 (Oxford University Press, 1997)

Brewer, Mike. *Kick-start your choir* (Faber Music, 1997)

Buchanan, Kate and Chadwick, Stephen. *Music Connections—Practical Music for all Primary Class Teachers* (Cramer Music, 1996)

Glennie, Evelyn and Cameron, Paul. *Beat it! African Dances* (Faber Music, 1997)

Glennie, Evelyn and Cameron, Paul. *Beat it! Caribbean Street Music* (Faber Music, 2000)

Jones, Kate. *Keeping your nerve!* (Faber Music, 2000)

Holdstock, Jan and Richards, Chris. *Sounds Topical*. Key Stage 1 (Oxford University Press, 1995)

Marsh, Lin. *Junior Songscape* (Faber Music, forthcoming)

Mills, Janet. *Music in the Primary School* (Cambridge University Press, 1991)

Odam, George; Arnold, Joan and Ley, Alison. *Sounds of Music*. Key Stage 1 and 2 (Nelson Thornes, 1996)

Swanwick, Keith. *A Basis for Music Education* (Routledge, 1979)

Taylor, Dorothy J. et al. *Targeting Music* (Schott & Co, 1995)

For singing books, try anything from the A&C Black catalogue, some of which have helpful tapes. My own personal favourite is *Flying Around*, by David Gadsby and Beatrice Harrop (1982)

CONFIDENCE-BOOSTING STRATEGIES
for choral directors and teachers

KICK-START YOUR CHOIR

Mike Brewer

with an introduction by John Rutter

FABER *ff* MUSIC

Kick-start your choir is for teachers, choral directors, church musicians—
anybody who directs a choir. It presents a treasure-trove of ideas distilled
from years of innovative work with singers of all ages.

Practical strategies are offered on almost every aspect of choral
directorship, including the voice in the classroom, getting young
people to sing, sound gestures and conducting. *Kick-start your
choir* is the indispensable handbook for the choral conductor.

"It should be acquired and read by every choir director." (*The Singer*)

ISBN 0-571-51749-8